50 Premium Beer Recipes

By: Kelly Johnson

Table of Contents

- Classic Lager
- Imperial Stout
- Belgian Witbier
- IPA (India Pale Ale)
- Porter
- Pale Ale
- Wheat Beer
- Pilsner
- Amber Ale
- Brown Ale
- Barleywine
- Saison
- Bock
- Cream Ale
- Dunkelweizen
- Schwarzbier
- Hefeweizen
- Tripel
- Dubbel
- Vienna Lager
- Rauchbier (Smoked Beer)
- Milk Stout
- Fruit Beer (with berries or citrus)
- Sour Ale (Gose, Berliner Weisse)
- Red Ale
- Imperial IPA
- Blonde Ale
- Rye Beer
- New England IPA (Hazy IPA)
- Double IPA
- Nitro Stout
- Baltic Porter
- Summer Ale
- Oktoberfest Lager
- Honey Ale

- Pumpkin Ale
- Black IPA
- Tropical Pale Ale
- Coconut Porter
- Chocolate Stout
- Coffee Ale
- Maple Brown Ale
- Bourbon Barrel-Aged Stout
- Lemon Pilsner
- Grapefruit IPA
- Chili Pepper Beer
- Grape Ale
- Spiced Winter Ale
- Tropical Wheat Beer
- Lemon Ginger Beer

Classic Lager

Ingredients:

- 8 lbs Pale Malt (2-row)
- 1 lb Munich Malt
- 0.5 lb Carapils Malt
- 1 oz Hallertau Hops (Bittering)
- 0.5 oz Saaz Hops (Flavoring)
- 1 Whirlfloc Tablet (optional, for clarity)
- 1.5 oz Saaz Hops (Aroma)
- Wyeast 1056 American Ale Yeast or similar lager yeast

Instructions:

1. **Mash**: Heat 3.5 gallons of water to 165°F (74°C). Add the grains and mash at 150°F (65.5°C) for 60 minutes. Stir occasionally. After 60 minutes, raise the temperature to 168°F (76°C) for a 10-minute mash out.
2. **Sparge**: Sparge with water heated to 168°F (76°C), collecting the wort until you have about 6.5 gallons of wort in your kettle.
3. **Boil**: Bring the wort to a boil. Once boiling, add the Hallertau hops and boil for 60 minutes. At the 45-minute mark, add the Saaz hops for flavor, and if desired, add a Whirlfloc tablet to help with clarity.
4. **Chill**: After the boil, chill the wort quickly to 70°F (21°C) using a wort chiller. Transfer the wort to the fermenter and aerate the wort by stirring vigorously.
5. **Fermentation**: Pitch the yeast into the cooled wort and ferment at 65°F (18°C) for 1 week. Then, lower the temperature to 45°F (7°C) and lager for 3-4 weeks.
6. **Packaging**: After lagering, transfer the beer into bottles or kegs, carbonate, and store at 35°F (1.5°C) until ready to enjoy.

Imperial Stout

Ingredients:

- 9 lbs Pale Malt
- 2 lbs Roasted Barley
- 1 lb Chocolate Malt
- 0.5 lb Black Patent Malt
- 1 lb Flaked Barley
- 1 oz East Kent Goldings Hops (Bittering)
- 1 oz Fuggle Hops (Flavoring)
- 1 Whirlfloc Tablet (optional)
- Wyeast 1098 British Ale Yeast or similar stout yeast

Instructions:

1. **Mash**: Heat 3.5 gallons of water to 165°F (74°C). Add the grains and mash at 154°F (68°C) for 60 minutes.
2. **Sparge**: Sparge with water at 168°F (76°C) to collect 6.5 gallons of wort.
3. **Boil**: Boil for 60 minutes, adding hops at the specified times.
4. **Chill**: Chill to 70°F (21°C) and pitch yeast.
5. **Fermentation**: Ferment at 65°F (18°C) for 1-2 weeks, then lager for 2-3 weeks.
6. **Packaging**: Package and carbonate.

Belgian Witbier

Ingredients:

- 5 lbs Pilsner Malt
- 3 lbs Wheat Malt
- 1 lb Flaked Wheat
- 1 oz Saaz Hops (Bittering)
- 0.5 oz Coriander Seed (Crushed)
- 1 oz Bitter Orange Peel
- Wyeast 3944 Belgian Witbier Yeast

Instructions:

1. **Mash**: Heat 3.5 gallons of water to 165°F (74°C) and mash at 152°F (67°C) for 60 minutes.
2. **Sparge**: Sparge and collect 6.5 gallons of wort.
3. **Boil**: Boil for 60 minutes, adding hops at the beginning and spices in the last 5 minutes.
4. **Chill**: Chill to 70°F (21°C), pitch yeast.
5. **Fermentation**: Ferment at 65°F (18°C) for 1-2 weeks.
6. **Packaging**: Package and carbonate.

IPA (India Pale Ale)

Ingredients:

- 9 lbs Pale Malt
- 1 lb Caramel Malt (40L)
- 1 oz Cascade Hops (Bittering)
- 2 oz Citra Hops (Flavoring)
- 2 oz Amarillo Hops (Aroma)
- Wyeast 1056 American Ale Yeast

Instructions:

1. **Mash**: Mash at 154°F (68°C) for 60 minutes.
2. **Sparge**: Sparge and collect 6 gallons of wort.
3. **Boil**: Boil for 60 minutes, adding hops at the specified times.
4. **Chill**: Chill to 70°F (21°C) and pitch yeast.
5. **Fermentation**: Ferment at 65°F (18°C) for 1-2 weeks.
6. **Packaging**: Package and carbonate.

Porter

Ingredients:

- 8 lbs Pale Malt
- 1 lb Chocolate Malt
- 0.5 lb Black Patent Malt
- 0.5 lb Crystal Malt (40L)
- 1 oz East Kent Goldings Hops (Bittering)
- 0.5 oz Fuggle Hops (Flavoring)
- Wyeast 1098 British Ale Yeast

Instructions:

1. **Mash**: Mash at 155°F (68°C) for 60 minutes.
2. **Sparge**: Sparge and collect 6 gallons of wort.
3. **Boil**: Boil for 60 minutes, adding hops at the specified times.
4. **Chill**: Chill to 70°F (21°C), pitch yeast.
5. **Fermentation**: Ferment at 65°F (18°C) for 1-2 weeks.
6. **Packaging**: Package and carbonate.

Pale Ale

Ingredients:

- 8 lbs Pale Malt
- 1 lb Caramel Malt (40L)
- 1 oz Cascade Hops (Bittering)
- 1 oz Amarillo Hops (Flavoring)
- 1 oz Centennial Hops (Aroma)
- Wyeast 1056 American Ale Yeast

Instructions:

1. **Mash**: Mash at 153°F (67°C) for 60 minutes.
2. **Sparge**: Sparge and collect 6 gallons of wort.
3. **Boil**: Boil for 60 minutes, adding hops at the specified times.
4. **Chill**: Chill to 70°F (21°C), pitch yeast.
5. **Fermentation**: Ferment at 65°F (18°C) for 1-2 weeks.
6. **Packaging**: Package and carbonate.

Wheat Beer

Ingredients:

- 6 lbs Wheat Malt
- 4 lbs Pilsner Malt
- 1 oz Hallertau Hops (Bittering)
- 0.5 oz Saaz Hops (Flavoring)
- Wyeast 3068 Weihenstephan Weizen Yeast

Instructions:

1. **Mash**: Mash at 152°F (67°C) for 60 minutes.
2. **Sparge**: Sparge and collect 6 gallons of wort.
3. **Boil**: Boil for 60 minutes, adding hops at the specified times.
4. **Chill**: Chill to 70°F (21°C), pitch yeast.
5. **Fermentation**: Ferment at 65°F (18°C) for 1-2 weeks.
6. **Packaging**: Package and carbonate.

Pilsner

Ingredients:

- 8 lbs Pilsner Malt
- 1 oz Saaz Hops (Bittering)
- 0.5 oz Saaz Hops (Flavoring)
- Wyeast 2124 Bohemian Pilsner Yeast

Instructions:

1. **Mash**: Mash at 150°F (66°C) for 60 minutes.
2. **Sparge**: Sparge and collect 6 gallons of wort.
3. **Boil**: Boil for 60 minutes, adding hops at the specified times.
4. **Chill**: Chill to 70°F (21°C), pitch yeast.
5. **Fermentation**: Ferment at 45°F (7°C) for 2-3 weeks.
6. **Packaging**: Package and carbonate.

Amber Ale

Ingredients:

- 7 lbs Pale Malt
- 1 lb Crystal Malt (40L)
- 0.5 lb Chocolate Malt
- 1 oz Cascade Hops (Bittering)
- 0.5 oz Amarillo Hops (Flavoring)
- Wyeast 1056 American Ale Yeast

Instructions:

1. **Mash**: Mash at 154°F (68°C) for 60 minutes.
2. **Sparge**: Sparge and collect 6 gallons of wort.
3. **Boil**: Boil for 60 minutes, adding hops at the specified times.
4. **Chill**: Chill to 70°F (21°C), pitch yeast.
5. **Fermentation**: Ferment at 65°F (18°C) for 1-2 weeks.
6. **Packaging**: Package and carbonate.

Brown Ale

Ingredients:

- 8 lbs Pale Malt
- 1 lb Caramel Malt (40L)
- 0.5 lb Chocolate Malt
- 1 oz East Kent Goldings Hops (Bittering)
- 1 oz Fuggle Hops (Flavoring)
- Wyeast 1098 British Ale Yeast

Instructions:

1. **Mash**: Mash at 154°F (68°C) for 60 minutes.
2. **Sparge**: Sparge and collect 6 gallons of wort.
3. **Boil**: Boil for 60 minutes, adding hops at the specified times.
4. **Chill**: Chill to 70°F (21°C), pitch yeast.
5. **Fermentation**: Ferment at 65°F (18°C) for 1-2 weeks.
6. **Packaging**: Package and carbonate.

Barleywine

Ingredients:

- 10 lbs Pale Malt
- 2 lbs Caramel Malt (60L)
- 1 lb Munich Malt
- 1 lb Special B Malt
- 1 oz Chinook Hops (Bittering)
- 1 oz Cascade Hops (Flavoring)
- Wyeast 1056 American Ale Yeast

Instructions:

1. **Mash**: Mash at 154°F (68°C) for 90 minutes.
2. **Sparge**: Sparge and collect 6 gallons of wort.
3. **Boil**: Boil for 90 minutes, adding hops at the specified times.
4. **Chill**: Chill to 70°F (21°C), pitch yeast.
5. **Fermentation**: Ferment at 65°F (18°C) for 2-3 weeks.
6. **Packaging**: Package and carbonate.

Saison

Ingredients:

- 8 lbs Pilsner Malt
- 1 lb Wheat Malt
- 1 lb Munich Malt
- 1 oz Saaz Hops (Bittering)
- 0.5 oz Styrian Golding Hops (Flavoring)
- Wyeast 3711 French Saison Yeast

Instructions:

1. **Mash**: Mash at 154°F (68°C) for 60 minutes.
2. **Sparge**: Sparge and collect 6 gallons of wort.
3. **Boil**: Boil for 60 minutes, adding hops at the specified times.
4. **Chill**: Chill to 70°F (21°C), pitch yeast.
5. **Fermentation**: Ferment at 70°F (21°C) for 1-2 weeks.
6. **Packaging**: Package and carbonate.

Bock

Ingredients:

- 8 lbs Munich Malt
- 4 lbs Pale Malt
- 1 lb Caramel Malt (40L)
- 1 oz Hallertau Hops (Bittering)
- Wyeast 2124 Bohemian Pilsner Yeast

Instructions:

1. **Mash**: Mash at 155°F (68°C) for 60 minutes.
2. **Sparge**: Sparge and collect 6 gallons of wort.
3. **Boil**: Boil for 60 minutes, adding hops at the beginning.
4. **Chill**: Chill to 70°F (21°C), pitch yeast.
5. **Fermentation**: Ferment at 50°F (10°C) for 2-3 weeks.
6. **Packaging**: Package and carbonate.

Cream Ale

Ingredients:

- 6 lbs Pale Malt
- 4 lbs Corn (Flaked)
- 1 oz Cascade Hops (Bittering)
- Wyeast 1056 American Ale Yeast

Instructions:

1. **Mash**: Mash at 150°F (65°C) for 60 minutes.
2. **Sparge**: Sparge and collect 6 gallons of wort.
3. **Boil**: Boil for 60 minutes, adding hops at the beginning.
4. **Chill**: Chill to 70°F (21°C), pitch yeast.
5. **Fermentation**: Ferment at 65°F (18°C) for 1-2 weeks.
6. **Packaging**: Package and carbonate.

Dunkelweizen

Ingredients:

- 5 lbs Wheat Malt
- 5 lbs Munich Malt
- 1 lb Chocolate Malt
- 1 oz Hallertau Hops (Bittering)
- Wyeast 3068 Weihenstephan Weizen Yeast

Instructions:

1. **Mash**: Mash at 152°F (67°C) for 60 minutes.
2. **Sparge**: Sparge and collect 6 gallons of wort.
3. **Boil**: Boil for 60 minutes, adding hops at the beginning.
4. **Chill**: Chill to 70°F (21°C), pitch yeast.
5. **Fermentation**: Ferment at 65°F (18°C) for 1-2 weeks.
6. **Packaging**: Package and carbonate.

Schwarzbier

Ingredients:

- 8 lbs Pale Malt
- 2 lbs Munich Malt
- 1 lb Caramel Malt (40L)
- 0.5 lb Black Patent Malt
- 1 oz Hallertau Hops (Bittering)
- Wyeast 2124 Bohemian Pilsner Yeast

Instructions:

1. **Mash**: Mash at 152°F (67°C) for 60 minutes.
2. **Sparge**: Sparge and collect 6 gallons of wort.
3. **Boil**: Boil for 60 minutes, adding hops at the beginning.
4. **Chill**: Chill to 70°F (21°C), pitch yeast.
5. **Fermentation**: Ferment at 50°F (10°C) for 2-3 weeks.
6. **Packaging**: Package and carbonate.

Hefeweizen

Ingredients:

- 6 lbs Wheat Malt
- 4 lbs Pale Malt
- 1 oz Hallertau Hops (Bittering)
- Wyeast 3068 Weihenstephan Weizen Yeast

Instructions:

1. **Mash**: Mash at 154°F (68°C) for 60 minutes.
2. **Sparge**: Sparge and collect 6 gallons of wort.
3. **Boil**: Boil for 60 minutes, adding hops at the beginning.
4. **Chill**: Chill to 70°F (21°C), pitch yeast.
5. **Fermentation**: Ferment at 65°F (18°C) for 1-2 weeks.
6. **Packaging**: Package and carbonate.

Tripel

Ingredients:

- 10 lbs Pilsner Malt
- 1 lb Candy Sugar (Belgian)
- 1 oz Saaz Hops (Bittering)
- Wyeast 3787 Trappist High Gravity Yeast

Instructions:

1. **Mash**: Mash at 152°F (67°C) for 60 minutes.
2. **Sparge**: Sparge and collect 6 gallons of wort.
3. **Boil**: Boil for 60 minutes, adding hops at the beginning.
4. **Chill**: Chill to 70°F (21°C), pitch yeast.
5. **Fermentation**: Ferment at 65°F (18°C) for 2-3 weeks.
6. **Packaging**: Package and carbonate.

Dubbel

Ingredients:

- 8 lbs Pilsner Malt
- 2 lbs Munich Malt
- 1 lb Belgian Dark Candi Sugar
- 1 oz Hallertau Hops (Bittering)
- Wyeast 1214 Belgian Ale Yeast

Instructions:

1. **Mash**: Mash at 154°F (68°C) for 60 minutes.
2. **Sparge**: Sparge and collect 6 gallons of wort.
3. **Boil**: Boil for 60 minutes, adding hops at the beginning.
4. **Chill**: Chill to 70°F (21°C), pitch yeast.
5. **Fermentation**: Ferment at 65°F (18°C) for 2-3 weeks.
6. **Packaging**: Package and carbonate.

Vienna Lager

Ingredients:

- 8 lbs Vienna Malt
- 1 lb Munich Malt
- 0.5 lb Caramel Malt (40L)
- 1 oz Hallertau Hops (Bittering)
- Wyeast 2206 Bavarian Lager Yeast

Instructions:

1. **Mash**: Mash at 150°F (66°C) for 60 minutes.
2. **Sparge**: Sparge and collect 6 gallons of wort.
3. **Boil**: Boil for 60 minutes, adding hops at the beginning.
4. **Chill**: Chill to 70°F (21°C), pitch yeast.
5. **Fermentation**: Ferment at 50°F (10°C) for 2-3 weeks.
6. **Packaging**: Package and carbonate.

Rauchbier (Smoked Beer)

Ingredients:

- 7 lbs Pilsner Malt
- 3 lbs Smoked Malt (e.g., Beechwood)
- 1 lb Munich Malt
- 1 oz Hallertau Hops (Bittering)
- Wyeast 2124 Bohemian Pilsner Yeast

Instructions:

1. **Mash**: Mash at 152°F (67°C) for 60 minutes.
2. **Sparge**: Sparge and collect 6 gallons of wort.
3. **Boil**: Boil for 60 minutes, adding hops at the beginning.
4. **Chill**: Chill to 70°F (21°C), pitch yeast.
5. **Fermentation**: Ferment at 50°F (10°C) for 2-3 weeks.
6. **Packaging**: Package and carbonate.

Milk Stout

Ingredients:

- 6 lbs Pale Malt
- 1 lb Chocolate Malt
- 1 lb Lactose (Milk Sugar)
- 0.5 lb Caramel Malt (40L)
- 1 oz East Kent Goldings Hops (Bittering)
- Wyeast 1028 London Ale Yeast

Instructions:

1. **Mash**: Mash at 154°F (68°C) for 60 minutes.
2. **Sparge**: Sparge and collect 6 gallons of wort.
3. **Boil**: Boil for 60 minutes, adding hops at the beginning.
4. **Chill**: Chill to 70°F (21°C), pitch yeast.
5. **Fermentation**: Ferment at 65°F (18°C) for 1-2 weeks.
6. **Packaging**: Package and carbonate.

Fruit Beer (with Berries or Citrus)

Ingredients:

- 7 lbs Pale Malt
- 1 lb Caramel Malt (40L)
- 1 lb Fruit (berries or citrus, such as raspberries or oranges)
- 1 oz Cascade Hops (Bittering)
- Wyeast 1056 American Ale Yeast

Instructions:

1. **Mash**: Mash at 152°F (67°C) for 60 minutes.
2. **Sparge**: Sparge and collect 6 gallons of wort.
3. **Boil**: Boil for 60 minutes, adding hops at the beginning.
4. **Add Fruit**: Add fruit during the last 10 minutes of the boil.
5. **Chill**: Chill to 70°F (21°C), pitch yeast.
6. **Fermentation**: Ferment at 65°F (18°C) for 1-2 weeks.
7. **Packaging**: Package and carbonate.

Sour Ale (Gose, Berliner Weisse)

Ingredients:

- 5 lbs Pilsner Malt
- 3 lbs Wheat Malt
- 1 oz Hallertau Hops (Bittering)
- 0.5 oz Coriander (for Gose)
- 1 oz Sea Salt (for Gose)
- Wyeast 1098 British Ale Yeast or a Sour Blend (for Berliner Weisse)

Instructions:

1. **Mash**: Mash at 152°F (67°C) for 60 minutes.
2. **Sparge**: Sparge and collect 6 gallons of wort.
3. **Boil**: Boil for 60 minutes, adding hops at the beginning.
4. **Add Coriander and Salt**: Add during the last 10 minutes of the boil if making Gose.
5. **Chill**: Chill to 70°F (21°C), pitch yeast.
6. **Fermentation**: Ferment at 65°F (18°C) for 1-2 weeks.
7. **Packaging**: Package and carbonate.

Red Ale

Ingredients:

- 8 lbs Pale Malt
- 1 lb Munich Malt
- 1 lb Caramel Malt (40L)
- 1 oz Cascade Hops (Bittering)
- Wyeast 1056 American Ale Yeast

Instructions:

1. **Mash**: Mash at 154°F (68°C) for 60 minutes.
2. **Sparge**: Sparge and collect 6 gallons of wort.
3. **Boil**: Boil for 60 minutes, adding hops at the beginning.
4. **Chill**: Chill to 70°F (21°C), pitch yeast.
5. **Fermentation**: Ferment at 65°F (18°C) for 1-2 weeks.
6. **Packaging**: Package and carbonate.

Imperial IPA

Ingredients:

- 10 lbs Pale Malt
- 1 lb Munich Malt
- 1 lb Caramel Malt (20L)
- 2 oz Cascade Hops (Bittering)
- 2 oz Centennial Hops (Flavoring)
- 1 oz Amarillo Hops (Aroma)
- Wyeast 1056 American Ale Yeast

Instructions:

1. **Mash**: Mash at 154°F (68°C) for 60 minutes.
2. **Sparge**: Sparge and collect 6 gallons of wort.
3. **Boil**: Boil for 60 minutes, adding hops at the specified times.
4. **Chill**: Chill to 70°F (21°C), pitch yeast.
5. **Fermentation**: Ferment at 65°F (18°C) for 1-2 weeks.
6. **Packaging**: Package and carbonate.

Blonde Ale

Ingredients:

- 6 lbs Pale Malt
- 1 lb Caramel Malt (20L)
- 0.5 lb Munich Malt
- 1 oz Cascade Hops (Bittering)
- Wyeast 1056 American Ale Yeast

Instructions:

1. **Mash**: Mash at 154°F (68°C) for 60 minutes.
2. **Sparge**: Sparge and collect 6 gallons of wort.
3. **Boil**: Boil for 60 minutes, adding hops at the beginning.
4. **Chill**: Chill to 70°F (21°C), pitch yeast.
5. **Fermentation**: Ferment at 65°F (18°C) for 1-2 weeks.
6. **Packaging**: Package and carbonate.

Rye Beer

Ingredients:

- 7 lbs Pale Malt
- 3 lbs Rye Malt
- 1 lb Munich Malt
- 1 oz Cascade Hops (Bittering)
- Wyeast 1056 American Ale Yeast

Instructions:

1. **Mash**: Mash at 154°F (68°C) for 60 minutes.
2. **Sparge**: Sparge and collect 6 gallons of wort.
3. **Boil**: Boil for 60 minutes, adding hops at the beginning.
4. **Chill**: Chill to 70°F (21°C), pitch yeast.
5. **Fermentation**: Ferment at 65°F (18°C) for 1-2 weeks.
6. **Packaging**: Package and carbonate.

New England IPA (Hazy IPA)

Ingredients:

- 8 lbs Pale Malt
- 2 lbs Wheat Malt
- 2 lbs Oats (Flaked)
- 1 oz Citra Hops (Bittering)
- 1 oz Mosaic Hops (Flavoring)
- 1 oz Simcoe Hops (Aroma)
- Wyeast 1056 American Ale Yeast

Instructions:

1. **Mash**: Mash at 154°F (68°C) for 60 minutes.
2. **Sparge**: Sparge and collect 6 gallons of wort.
3. **Boil**: Boil for 60 minutes, adding hops at the specified times.
4. **Chill**: Chill to 70°F (21°C), pitch yeast.
5. **Fermentation**: Ferment at 65°F (18°C) for 1-2 weeks.
6. **Packaging**: Package and carbonate.

Double IPA

Ingredients:

- 12 lbs Pale Malt
- 1 lb Munich Malt
- 1 lb Caramel Malt (20L)
- 2 oz Simcoe Hops (Bittering)
- 2 oz Amarillo Hops (Flavoring)
- 2 oz Citra Hops (Aroma)
- Wyeast 1056 American Ale Yeast

Instructions:

1. **Mash**: Mash at 154°F (68°C) for 60 minutes.
2. **Sparge**: Sparge and collect 6 gallons of wort.
3. **Boil**: Boil for 60 minutes, adding hops at the specified times.
4. **Chill**: Chill to 70°F (21°C), pitch yeast.
5. **Fermentation**: Ferment at 65°F (18°C) for 1-2 weeks.
6. **Packaging**: Package and carbonate.

Nitro Stout

Ingredients:

- 8 lbs Pale Malt
- 2 lbs Roasted Barley
- 1 lb Chocolate Malt
- 0.5 lb Caramel Malt (40L)
- 1 oz East Kent Goldings Hops (Bittering)
- Wyeast 1084 Irish Ale Yeast

Instructions:

1. **Mash**: Mash at 154°F (68°C) for 60 minutes.
2. **Sparge**: Sparge and collect 6 gallons of wort.
3. **Boil**: Boil for 60 minutes, adding hops at the beginning.
4. **Chill**: Chill to 70°F (21°C), pitch yeast.
5. **Fermentation**: Ferment at 65°F (18°C) for 1-2 weeks.
6. **Nitrogenation**: Once fermentation is complete, force carbonate with nitrogen gas and serve on nitro tap.

Baltic Porter

Ingredients:

- 8 lbs Pale Malt
- 2 lbs Munich Malt
- 1 lb Chocolate Malt
- 1 lb Black Patent Malt
- 0.5 lb Caramel Malt (40L)
- 1 oz Saaz Hops (Bittering)
- Wyeast 2278 Czech Pilsner Yeast

Instructions:

1. **Mash**: Mash at 154°F (68°C) for 60 minutes.
2. **Sparge**: Sparge and collect 6 gallons of wort.
3. **Boil**: Boil for 60 minutes, adding hops at the beginning.
4. **Chill**: Chill to 70°F (21°C), pitch yeast.
5. **Fermentation**: Ferment at 50°F (10°C) for 2-3 weeks.
6. **Packaging**: Package and carbonate.

Summer Ale

Ingredients:

- 6 lbs Pale Malt
- 2 lbs Wheat Malt
- 1 lb Caramel Malt (20L)
- 1 oz Cascade Hops (Bittering)
- 1 oz Citra Hops (Aroma)
- Wyeast 1056 American Ale Yeast

Instructions:

1. **Mash**: Mash at 154°F (68°C) for 60 minutes.
2. **Sparge**: Sparge and collect 6 gallons of wort.
3. **Boil**: Boil for 60 minutes, adding hops at the beginning.
4. **Chill**: Chill to 70°F (21°C), pitch yeast.
5. **Fermentation**: Ferment at 65°F (18°C) for 1-2 weeks.
6. **Packaging**: Package and carbonate.

Oktoberfest Lager

Ingredients:

- 8 lbs Pale Malt
- 3 lbs Munich Malt
- 1 lb Caramel Malt (40L)
- 1 oz Hallertau Hops (Bittering)
- Wyeast 2206 Bavarian Lager Yeast

Instructions:

1. **Mash**: Mash at 154°F (68°C) for 60 minutes.
2. **Sparge**: Sparge and collect 6 gallons of wort.
3. **Boil**: Boil for 60 minutes, adding hops at the beginning.
4. **Chill**: Chill to 50°F (10°C), pitch yeast.
5. **Fermentation**: Ferment at 50°F (10°C) for 4-6 weeks.
6. **Packaging**: Package and carbonate.

Honey Ale

Ingredients:

- 7 lbs Pale Malt
- 1 lb Honey (added to the boil)
- 1 lb Caramel Malt (20L)
- 1 oz Cascade Hops (Bittering)
- Wyeast 1056 American Ale Yeast

Instructions:

1. **Mash**: Mash at 154°F (68°C) for 60 minutes.
2. **Sparge**: Sparge and collect 6 gallons of wort.
3. **Boil**: Boil for 60 minutes, adding hops at the beginning.
4. **Add Honey**: Add honey during the last 15 minutes of the boil.
5. **Chill**: Chill to 70°F (21°C), pitch yeast.
6. **Fermentation**: Ferment at 65°F (18°C) for 1-2 weeks.
7. **Packaging**: Package and carbonate.

Pumpkin Ale

Ingredients:

- 6 lbs Pale Malt
- 2 lbs Pumpkin Puree (added to the boil)
- 1 lb Caramel Malt (20L)
- 1 oz Saaz Hops (Bittering)
- 2 tsp Pumpkin Pie Spice (added in the last 10 minutes)
- Wyeast 1056 American Ale Yeast

Instructions:

1. **Mash**: Mash at 154°F (68°C) for 60 minutes.
2. **Sparge**: Sparge and collect 6 gallons of wort.
3. **Boil**: Boil for 60 minutes, adding hops at the beginning.
4. **Add Pumpkin**: Add pumpkin puree during the last 15 minutes of the boil.
5. **Add Spices**: Add pumpkin pie spice during the last 10 minutes of the boil.
6. **Chill**: Chill to 70°F (21°C), pitch yeast.
7. **Fermentation**: Ferment at 65°F (18°C) for 1-2 weeks.
8. **Packaging**: Package and carbonate.

Black IPA

Ingredients:

- 7 lbs Pale Malt
- 1 lb Black Malt
- 1 lb Caramel Malt (40L)
- 1 oz Simcoe Hops (Bittering)
- 1 oz Centennial Hops (Flavoring)
- 1 oz Amarillo Hops (Aroma)
- Wyeast 1056 American Ale Yeast

Instructions:

1. **Mash**: Mash at 154°F (68°C) for 60 minutes.
2. **Sparge**: Sparge and collect 6 gallons of wort.
3. **Boil**: Boil for 60 minutes, adding hops at the beginning.
4. **Chill**: Chill to 70°F (21°C), pitch yeast.
5. **Fermentation**: Ferment at 65°F (18°C) for 1-2 weeks.
6. **Packaging**: Package and carbonate.

Tropical Pale Ale

Ingredients:

- 7 lbs Pale Malt
- 2 lbs Munich Malt
- 0.5 lb Caramel Malt (40L)
- 1 oz Citra Hops (Bittering)
- 1 oz Amarillo Hops (Flavoring)
- 1 oz Mosaic Hops (Aroma)
- 1 lb Tropical Fruit (e.g., pineapple, mango, or passion fruit)
- Wyeast 1056 American Ale Yeast

Instructions:

1. **Mash**: Mash at 154°F (68°C) for 60 minutes.
2. **Sparge**: Sparge and collect 6 gallons of wort.
3. **Boil**: Boil for 60 minutes, adding hops at the specified times.
4. **Add Fruit**: Add tropical fruit during the last 10 minutes of the boil.
5. **Chill**: Chill to 70°F (21°C), pitch yeast.
6. **Fermentation**: Ferment at 65°F (18°C) for 1-2 weeks.
7. **Packaging**: Package and carbonate.

Coconut Porter

Ingredients:

- 6 lbs Pale Malt
- 2 lbs Chocolate Malt
- 1 lb Caramel Malt (40L)
- 1 lb Flaked Barley
- 1 oz East Kent Goldings Hops (Bittering)
- 1 lb Shredded Coconut (added after fermentation)
- Wyeast 1028 London Ale Yeast

Instructions:

1. **Mash**: Mash at 154°F (68°C) for 60 minutes.
2. **Sparge**: Sparge and collect 6 gallons of wort.
3. **Boil**: Boil for 60 minutes, adding hops at the beginning.
4. **Chill**: Chill to 70°F (21°C), pitch yeast.
5. **Fermentation**: Ferment at 65°F (18°C) for 1-2 weeks.
6. **Add Coconut**: Add shredded coconut to fermenter during secondary fermentation.
7. **Packaging**: Package and carbonate.

Chocolate Stout

Ingredients:

- 8 lbs Pale Malt
- 1 lb Chocolate Malt
- 0.5 lb Black Patent Malt
- 1 lb Caramel Malt (40L)
- 1 oz East Kent Goldings Hops (Bittering)
- 4 oz Cocoa Nibs (added at the end of the boil)
- Wyeast 1028 London Ale Yeast

Instructions:

1. **Mash**: Mash at 154°F (68°C) for 60 minutes.
2. **Sparge**: Sparge and collect 6 gallons of wort.
3. **Boil**: Boil for 60 minutes, adding hops at the beginning.
4. **Add Cocoa**: Add cocoa nibs during the last 10 minutes of the boil.
5. **Chill**: Chill to 70°F (21°C), pitch yeast.
6. **Fermentation**: Ferment at 65°F (18°C) for 1-2 weeks.
7. **Packaging**: Package and carbonate.

Coffee Ale

Ingredients:

- 6 lbs Pale Malt
- 2 lbs Caramel Malt (40L)
- 0.5 lb Chocolate Malt
- 1 oz Cascade Hops (Bittering)
- 4 oz Fresh Coffee Grounds (added after fermentation)
- Wyeast 1056 American Ale Yeast

Instructions:

1. **Mash**: Mash at 154°F (68°C) for 60 minutes.
2. **Sparge**: Sparge and collect 6 gallons of wort.
3. **Boil**: Boil for 60 minutes, adding hops at the beginning.
4. **Chill**: Chill to 70°F (21°C), pitch yeast.
5. **Fermentation**: Ferment at 65°F (18°C) for 1-2 weeks.
6. **Add Coffee**: After fermentation, add freshly brewed or cold-brewed coffee to the fermenter.
7. **Packaging**: Package and carbonate.

Maple Brown Ale

Ingredients:

- 7 lbs Pale Malt
- 2 lbs Munich Malt
- 1 lb Caramel Malt (40L)
- 1 lb Chocolate Malt
- 1 oz Fuggle Hops (Bittering)
- 8 oz Maple Syrup (added during fermentation)
- Wyeast 1028 London Ale Yeast

Instructions:

1. **Mash**: Mash at 154°F (68°C) for 60 minutes.
2. **Sparge**: Sparge and collect 6 gallons of wort.
3. **Boil**: Boil for 60 minutes, adding hops at the beginning.
4. **Add Maple Syrup**: Add maple syrup in the last 10 minutes of the boil.
5. **Chill**: Chill to 70°F (21°C), pitch yeast.
6. **Fermentation**: Ferment at 65°F (18°C) for 1-2 weeks.
7. **Packaging**: Package and carbonate.

Bourbon Barrel-Aged Stout

Ingredients:

- 8 lbs Pale Malt
- 1 lb Chocolate Malt
- 1 lb Black Patent Malt
- 1 lb Caramel Malt (40L)
- 0.5 lb Roasted Barley
- 1 oz East Kent Goldings Hops (Bittering)
- 4 oz Bourbon-soaked Oak Chips (added in secondary fermentation)
- Wyeast 1028 London Ale Yeast

Instructions:

1. **Mash**: Mash at 154°F (68°C) for 60 minutes.
2. **Sparge**: Sparge and collect 6 gallons of wort.
3. **Boil**: Boil for 60 minutes, adding hops at the beginning.
4. **Chill**: Chill to 70°F (21°C), pitch yeast.
5. **Fermentation**: Ferment at 65°F (18°C) for 1-2 weeks.
6. **Add Oak Chips**: After primary fermentation, add bourbon-soaked oak chips to secondary fermentation.
7. **Aging**: Age for 4-6 weeks for maximum flavor extraction.
8. **Packaging**: Package and carbonate.

Lemon Pilsner

Ingredients:

- 6 lbs Pilsner Malt
- 1 lb Munich Malt
- 0.5 lb Caramel Malt (20L)
- 1 oz Saaz Hops (Bittering)
- Zest of 2 Lemons (added during the boil)
- 1 oz Lemondrop Hops (Flavoring)
- Wyeast 2124 Bohemian Lager Yeast

Instructions:

1. **Mash**: Mash at 154°F (68°C) for 60 minutes.
2. **Sparge**: Sparge and collect 6 gallons of wort.
3. **Boil**: Boil for 60 minutes, adding hops at the beginning.
4. **Add Lemon Zest**: Add lemon zest during the last 10 minutes of the boil.
5. **Chill**: Chill to 50°F (10°C), pitch yeast.
6. **Fermentation**: Ferment at 50°F (10°C) for 2-3 weeks.
7. **Packaging**: Package and carbonate.

Grapefruit IPA

Ingredients:

- 8 lbs Pale Malt
- 1 lb Munich Malt
- 1 lb Caramel Malt (40L)
- 1 oz Centennial Hops (Bittering)
- 1 oz Amarillo Hops (Flavoring)
- 1 oz Citra Hops (Dry Hopping)
- Zest of 2 Grapefruits (added during fermentation)
- Wyeast 1056 American Ale Yeast

Instructions:

1. **Mash**: Mash at 154°F (68°C) for 60 minutes.
2. **Sparge**: Sparge and collect 6 gallons of wort.
3. **Boil**: Boil for 60 minutes, adding hops at the beginning.
4. **Add Grapefruit Zest**: Add grapefruit zest in secondary fermentation after the initial fermentation is complete.
5. **Fermentation**: Ferment at 65°F (18°C) for 1-2 weeks.
6. **Dry Hopping**: Dry hop with Citra hops during the final 5-7 days of fermentation.
7. **Packaging**: Package and carbonate.

Chili Pepper Beer

Ingredients:

- 6 lbs Pale Malt
- 2 lbs Caramel Malt (20L)
- 1 oz Cascade Hops (Bittering)
- 2-3 Dried Chili Peppers (Add during the boil or fermentation, based on desired heat)
- 1 oz Jalapeño Hops (Flavoring)
- Wyeast 1056 American Ale Yeast

Instructions:

1. **Mash**: Mash at 154°F (68°C) for 60 minutes.
2. **Sparge**: Sparge and collect 6 gallons of wort.
3. **Boil**: Boil for 60 minutes, adding hops at the beginning.
4. **Add Chili Peppers**: Add dried chili peppers during the boil or after fermentation to control heat levels.
5. **Fermentation**: Ferment at 65°F (18°C) for 1-2 weeks.
6. **Dry Hopping**: Optionally, dry hop with Jalapeño hops for an additional spicy kick.
7. **Packaging**: Package and carbonate.

Grape Ale

Ingredients:

- 7 lbs Pale Malt
- 1 lb Wheat Malt
- 1 lb Caramel Malt (40L)
- 1 oz Hallertau Hops (Bittering)
- 2 lbs Fresh Grapes (crushed, added during fermentation)
- 1 tsp Irish Moss (Optional, for clarity)
- Wyeast 1056 American Ale Yeast

Instructions:

1. **Mash**: Mash at 154°F (68°C) for 60 minutes.
2. **Sparge**: Sparge and collect 6 gallons of wort.
3. **Boil**: Boil for 60 minutes, adding hops at the beginning.
4. **Add Grapes**: Crush fresh grapes and add them during the fermentation process after primary fermentation.
5. **Fermentation**: Ferment at 65°F (18°C) for 1-2 weeks.
6. **Packaging**: Package and carbonate.

Spiced Winter Ale

Ingredients:

- 6 lbs Pale Malt
- 2 lbs Munich Malt
- 1 lb Caramel Malt (40L)
- 1 oz Saaz Hops (Bittering)
- 1 oz Cinnamon Stick (Add during the boil)
- 1 tsp Ground Ginger (Add during the boil)
- 1 oz Orange Peel (Add during the boil)
- 2 Whole Cloves (Add during the boil)
- Wyeast 1098 British Ale Yeast

Instructions:

1. **Mash**: Mash at 154°F (68°C) for 60 minutes.
2. **Sparge**: Sparge and collect 6 gallons of wort.
3. **Boil**: Boil for 60 minutes, adding hops and spices during the last 15 minutes.
4. **Fermentation**: Ferment at 65°F (18°C) for 1-2 weeks.
5. **Packaging**: Package and carbonate.

Tropical Wheat Beer

Ingredients:

- 6 lbs Wheat Malt
- 4 lbs Pale Malt
- 0.5 lb Caramel Malt (20L)
- 1 oz Amarillo Hops (Bittering)
- 1 lb Mango (Pureed, added during fermentation)
- 1 lb Pineapple (Pureed, added during fermentation)
- Wyeast 1010 American Wheat Yeast

Instructions:

1. **Mash**: Mash at 154°F (68°C) for 60 minutes.
2. **Sparge**: Sparge and collect 6 gallons of wort.
3. **Boil**: Boil for 60 minutes, adding hops at the beginning.
4. **Add Tropical Fruits**: Add pureed mango and pineapple to the fermenter after the primary fermentation is complete.
5. **Fermentation**: Ferment at 65°F (18°C) for 1-2 weeks.
6. **Packaging**: Package and carbonate.

Lemon Ginger Beer

Ingredients:

- 6 lbs Pale Malt
- 2 lbs Wheat Malt
- 1 oz Saaz Hops (Bittering)
- 1 oz Fresh Ginger (Grated, added during the boil)
- Zest of 2 Lemons (added during the boil)
- 1 oz Lemon Juice (added after fermentation)
- Wyeast 1056 American Ale Yeast

Instructions:

1. **Mash**: Mash at 154°F (68°C) for 60 minutes.
2. **Sparge**: Sparge and collect 6 gallons of wort.
3. **Boil**: Boil for 60 minutes, adding hops, lemon zest, and grated ginger during the boil.
4. **Chill**: Chill to 70°F (21°C), pitch yeast.
5. **Fermentation**: Ferment at 65°F (18°C) for 1-2 weeks.
6. **Add Lemon Juice**: After fermentation, add lemon juice for added freshness.
7. **Packaging**: Package and carbonate.